cover TO cover

Habakkuk

CHOOSING GOD'S WAY

CWR

Steve Bishop

Contents

Introduction

Decisions are integral to daily life, and also the long-term future. Of course, most of the choices we make are relatively hassle-free. What should we buy for lunch? Is it cold enough to wear a jacket? Shall I take the bus or the train? What shall I read? (Hopefully the answer to that last question is to pick up one of these *Cover to Cover Bible Study* guides!)

Some choices, however, have greater significance but are unlikely to arise as often and so provide little or no past experience to draw on, in order to reach a decision. Educational courses, relationships, accommodation, health issues and financial commitments may all constitute such life-changing choices. When assessing our options in these areas, our limited knowledge of the subject together with our personal attitude and temperament is all we have to make major decisions.

The Bible in general, and the Old Testament in particular, includes much historical narrative… but with a difference! For many people history is viewed as a list of dates, monarchs, presidents, battles and inventions. This may lead to the conclusion that 'history is bunk' (according to car entrepreneur, Henry Ford) – uninteresting and irrelevant. The contents of the Old Testament, which focused on events and locations many millennia ago and many miles away, may mean that even some Christians hold the same view.

However, if we were to step back from that 'irrelevant' standpoint, we may come to hold a different opinion. History is about *people,* many just like ourselves. Although their outward circumstances may contrast with our own, they still had to face life as we do with its many problems. Like us they had to contend with stress, pressure, hopes, fears, disappointments, uncertainties and uncontrollable circumstances. They also were faced with choices, probably possessing few facts to help them.

In particular, the Israelites had to cope with periods of instability and inadequate resources which, understandably, affected their personal lives and decision-making. Slavery in Egypt, wilderness wanderings and conflict in the Promised Land meant that only a few generations were blessed with periods of peace and prosperity.

Joshua, instrumental in leading God's people into their homeland, had warned them of the need to 'choose for yourselves this day whom you will serve' (Josh. 24:15). Choices were beginning to kick in. The confident response back to Joshua was that the people would follow God, but this proved to be hollow. In later years the people decided to abandon God. 'Then the Israelites did evil in the eyes of the LORD and served the Baals. They forsook the LORD, the God of their ancestors, who had brought them out of Egypt' (Judg. 2:11–12).

A tedious cycle of events then followed. God raised up a succession of judges (leaders like Gideon and Samson) who would, against heavy odds, rescue the people from their enemies – who God had allowed to oppress them as a means of discipline. The nation would then decide to turn back to God, only to choose to abandon Him again and follow other gods (seemingly more attractive and beneficial). This sequence was repeated until the leadership of Samuel, when the people made the decision to be like the surrounding nations and have a king to lead them.

The choice that the people made to ask for a king 'displeased' Samuel the judge–prophet. God pointed out that it was He (the Lord) who was actually being 'rejected' by this decision (1 Sam. 8:6,7). Nevertheless, God's appointment of Saul as Israel's first monarch seemed to work well... initially. But then Saul himself started to made decisions – unwise ones with disastrous results. Sadly this started a trend with following kings. Although succeeded by King David (and then his son Solomon) who followed

God's ways, the nation of Israel fragmented. The northern ten tribes chose to separate themselves from the southern ones. They set up their own dynastic line of monarchs and religious worship. To a man, their leaders 'did evil in the eyes of the LORD' (2 Kings 15:8,9).

Those ten tribes, under the name of 'Israel', were finally overrun in 720 BC by the Assyrian superpower of that time. This left the tribes of Benjamin and Judah ('Judah' being the name of these two tribes now combining to form a national entity). Their successive leaders were kings of varying qualities. Some chose to follow God while others turned their back on Him. It was in this period of international instability and, for the ordinary person, insecurity and uncertainty, that God empowered prophets. These men included Isaiah and Jeremiah, who brought God's messages to both leaders and the general population.

There were other prophets who also revealed God's perspective to the nation of Judah, now isolated and threatened. Habakkuk was one of these, although nothing is known of his background or personal circumstances. What does emerge is that he was someone facing confusion and choices – as we do today. His apparent obscurity and powerlessness in the circumstances of life are again further aspects with which we would identify. These different pressures confronting Habakkuk would be 'boxes' that we could also 'tick'.

So we shall be looking at some features of Habakkuk's prophecy, seeing how they connect with ourselves and our own choices in following God. The key decision that this prophet had to face was choosing to place his confidence in God, despite outward circumstances. This is relevant to ourselves… so be prepared to make some hard decisions!

WEEK ONE

Complaining

Icebreaker

Draw up a list of organisations and businesses that you have regular contact with, and which provide formal channels for addressing complaints and grievances. What are the different means of contact by which such disputes can be lodged and pursued?

Bible Readings

- Habakkuk 1:1–4
- Psalm 142
- Isaiah 40:9–31
- Lamentations 3:39–42
- Mark 4:35–41
- Romans 12:12

Opening Our Eyes

The details were quite clear. Reading through the pages of some insurance documentation that I'd been sent revealed that the various aspects of the package on offer were comprehensively explained. One of these was headed: 'How do I complain?' The contact information and steps required in order to do this were clearly provided. This was similar to the way in which 'service providers' of all shapes and sizes are now geared to deal with customer dissatisfaction. From personal experience, having worked in a high-profile government department dealing with disputes connected to welfare payments, this was familiar territory from the receiving end!

However, the decision to complain and follow a grievance procedure is not a twenty-first-century phenomenon! The Bible records many examples. It seems to be our 'default' position as people. So when we read the opening verses of Habakkuk's prophecy (Hab. 1:1–4) and find him voicing some serious complaints, we are not surprised... except for possibly three factors.

State of affairs
The first of these is that the person who's engaged in this 'rant' is the prophet himself, seemingly doing so as part of his 'official' duties. We might have expected him to maintain an element of decorum, issuing a reasoned statement deploring the state of affairs and requiring action, all performed with an air of 'spokesperson' impartiality. But it's quite clear that Habakkuk is letting it all out, regardless of his role. The word 'prophecy' (v1) possibly meant 'burden' in the original Hebrew. Habakkuk was therefore simply responding to the weights upon his mind, emotions and spirit. Jeremiah, Ezekiel and other prophets were similar in the way their emotions clearly evidenced a response to the grievous circumstances around them (see Lam. 3 and Ezek. 3:14).

Habakkuk's passions had been aroused by the state of affairs that he was witnessing in the country of Judah at that time. Violence, conflict, a paralysed and perverse judicial system, oppression of the poor and righteous were all clearly evident. It's reckoned that these events were occurring during the reign of King Jehoiakim, described as doing evil, 'in the eyes of the LORD' (2 Chron. 36:5).

The decision of the people of Judah to act in these ways was bad enough. But what caused Habakkuk even greater grief was God's response. He appeared to be totally unmoved and inactive with regard to what was taking place. This was despite the prophet's sustained and heartfelt calling to Him for help. So this second factor is also important – God seemed to have gone AWOL. Habakkuk was complaining to Him and asking, in essence, 'What's going on?'

Being 'real'

But God was not fazed either by Habakkuk's reaction to circumstances or to the events themselves. This whole prophecy is unique in that it contains no direct message to either the people or their national leaders. It is set out as a dialogue – of an intense nature – between Habakkuk and God. We, in a sense, are eavesdropping on a highly charged one-to-one. This brings us to the third factor that's important to note. Habakkuk was being very 'real' about how he felt and what he perceived, together with the confusion that this all generated. His decision to bring this to God may not be packaged very well in our view. But it's an approach that would finally result in Habakkuk realising that he needed to choose God's way and decide to trust in Him – steps with which we can also identify.

Discussion Starters

1. What do these verses in Habakkuk teach us about prayer and relationship with God?

_____

_____

_____

_____

_____

2. What was Habakkuk's attitude to what was happening around him?

_____

_____

_____

_____

_____

3. The psalmist also wrote about complaining to God (Psa. 142). In what ways can his words help us identify with the personal nature of that complaint?

_____

_____

_____

_____

_____

4. Why is the element of powerlessness indicated in Psalm 142 (also in Habakkuk) so important in complaining to God?

_____

_____

_____

_____

_____

5. In what ways does the psalmist acknowledge that only God can resolve the issues that confront him? Why did it help the psalmist to take this approach?

_____

_____

_____

_____

_____

6. God made the Israelites aware that He'd heard their complaint (Isa. 40:27). What was the difference between this and previous complaints made by Habakkuk and the psalmist? Why did God draw attention to what He overheard?

_____

_____

_____

_____

_____

7. What contrast did God, through Isaiah's message, make with regard to Himself and other 'gods' (Isa. 40:18–26)? Why was this helpful to those complainers?

_____

_____

_____

_____

_____

8. In what ways can complaining reflect our lack of confidence in God? What choices could this lead us to make when thinking through our complaints to God (see Lam. 3:39–42)?

_____

_____

_____

_____

Personal Application

Facing up to adverse circumstances that impact us in a personal way (as was Habakkuk's experience) is an appropriate and spiritual response. Bringing them to God, even though He is fully aware of events, is also the right thing to do. We are instructed to be 'patient in affliction, faithful in prayer' (Rom. 12:12). However, even if we approach God in a complaining attitude, mixed with confusion, He understands our makeup and will patiently continue to help us grow spiritually, beyond our initial reaction.

Seeing Jesus in the Scriptures

This account in Habakkuk was not the only recorded occasion when the finger of complaint and accusation was pointed at God. The disciples were in a boat that was engulfed in a seismic storm while en route to the other side of the Sea of Galilee. Jesus, God become flesh, was asleep in the stern. Fearful of being overwhelmed and losing their lives, the disciples woke Him up with the complaint: 'Teacher, don't you care if we drown?' (Mark 4:38). Just as Habakkuk had experienced, God was neither ignorant nor powerless in regard to those dark and threatening circumstances. The disciples were subsequently reminded of their need for faith and trust.

WEEK TWO

Caught out

Icebreaker

Reflect upon a surprise gift that you may have received. List the various elements that may have contributed towards it being a surprise.

Bible Readings

- Habakkuk 1:5–11
- Judges 6:11–24; 7:1–8
- Isaiah 55:6–13
- Acts 9:10–18
- Acts 12:1–17
- Ephesians 3:14–21

Opening Our Eyes

'Managing expectations' is a phrase that's commonly used. A friend brought this up in conversation, describing someone who'd joined her church. This person had high hopes of her new spiritual family, but some expectations were not necessarily well-founded.

This is likely to be an attitude that we all encounter. Whatever the circumstances – for example, at work, in relationships, during medical treatment or on holiday – it's probable that we hold some preconceptions of what these events will be like. These may be based on recommendations, website reviews, a 'glass half full' approach, or simply concluding that, 'Things aren't good now, so they can't possibly get any worse.'

Perhaps Habakkuk shared that mentality when he complained to God. Having presented the list of issues that had been such a burden to him, the narrative abruptly stops. Without, it seems, any pause, God replied. The verses that follow contain information that totally surprised the prophet. Habakkuk was told that God had actually been at work. He was going to be, 'raising up the Babylonians' (1:5) as the means of answering that complaint, bringing discipline to the nation of Judah. In essence, this 'superpower' would be invading the country and taking the inhabitants into exile because of their spiritual rebellion.

God was quite aware and clear about the actions and attitude of those Babylonians whom He was about to release upon Judah. They were described as 'ruthless and impetuous... feared and dreaded... a law to themselves and [who] promote their own honour' (1:6–7). Their military prowess and track record was not in doubt. Habakkuk was having it clearly spelt out regarding future events. As Habakkuk listened, one could imagine his eyes widening and jaw dropping as he took on board what was being described.

Habakkuk, as we shall see, held certain conceptions about God and how He should act. This is a very human trait. Either consciously or otherwise, we all have certain expectations regarding God. But the response which Habakkuk now faced was a total surprise. God was working well 'outside the box'.

God's plan of action should not, actually, have been so unexpected. His selection of the Jewish nation as those through whom He would work and ultimately bring salvation to the world had been described generations previously. This selection by God was not an obvious one to those who may have been looking on. Moses had explained: 'The LORD your God has chosen you out of all the peoples on the face of the earth to be his people, his treasured possession. The LORD did not set his affection upon you and choose you because you were more numerous than other peoples, for you were the fewest of all peoples' (Deut. 7:6–7). Similarly, when the need for discipline arose then, God had previously allowed various pagan people-groups and terrorists to attack and oppress the Israelites. The book of Judges records a substantial list of them, including the Moabites, Canaanites, Midianites, Ammorites and Philistines.

God's unexpected response to Habakkuk's complaint also introduced an unforeseen prospect. This was that the situation was going to get worse before it got better. Unlike other occasions, the people of God were not going to see a divine reprieve from an overwhelming threat. But there was one other surprise – God's opening declaration: 'I am raising up' (1:6). Everything that was going to take place was with His full knowledge and under His ultimate authority. Such a fact was to prove foundational in Habakkuk subsequently choosing to place his confidence in God. But, like us, he first had to understand more about God's ways.

Discussion Starters

1. Why do you think that God's response to Habakkuk involved a description of the Babylonians and their characteristics in such detail? How can this relate to us?

_____

_____

_____

_____

_____

2. In what way did God alert Habakkuk to this surprise information? How can passages such as Isaiah 55:6–13 and Ephesians 3:14–21 prepare us for God's surprise action?

_____

_____

_____

_____

_____

3. Why was Gideon surprised at being appointed judge and deliverer (Judg. 6:11–16)? How can this encourage us?

_____

_____

_____

_____

_____

4. What happened to make things seem worse for Gideon before they got better (Judg. 7:1–8)? What can this teach us?

_____

_____

_____

_____

_____

5. Why was Ananias so surprised at God's instruction (Acts 9:10–18)? What does his obedience show us?

_____

_____

_____

_____

_____

6. What was the reaction of the praying church to the release of Peter (Acts 12:13–15)? What does this indicate about their praying – and our own?

_____

_____

_____

_____

_____

7. How does the apostle Paul explain the surprising choices of God in respect of those whom He calls (1 Cor. 1:26–29)? How should this affect our evangelism and witnessing?

_____

_____

_____

_____

_____

8. How should we respond to Paul's description of God doing more than we imagine (Eph. 3:14–21)?

_____

_____

_____

_____

_____

Personal Application

Our relationship with God is, inevitably, a journey of learning and revelation. Like Habakkuk we are sharing in what God is doing to forward and build up His work on this earth. There may be times when we have some understanding of what this probably means. But there are other occasions when we are, figuratively speaking, standing alongside Habakkuk in surprise-mode. God's work, either in our personal lives or in the situations around us, sometimes does not make sense. That's part of the 'learning curve' in helping us know God better and trust Him more deeply.

Seeing Jesus in the Scriptures

Jesus' ministry on earth frequently involved Him teaching aspects of God's kingdom that surprised His hearers. On one occasion it was recorded: 'The disciples were amazed at his words... The disciples were even more amazed' (Mark 10:24–26). His miraculous interventions also brought about surprised reactions. When facing the tomb of His friend Lazarus, He instructed that the stone be removed. The response was one of incredulity: 'But Lord... by this time there is a bad odour' (John 11:39). But the end result was resurrection from the dead. God's words and actions at the time of Habakkuk were consistent with this subsequent ministry of Jesus that it foreshadowed, revealing the ultimate power of God in every situation.

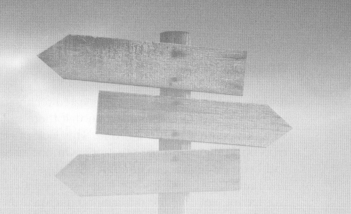

WEEK THREE

Confusion

Icebreaker

List the various aspects of a long journey that could (or perhaps have in the past!) spoil plans and cause it to be adversely affected, bringing overall confusion.

Bible Readings

- Habakkuk 1:12–17
- Psalm 31
- Psalm 77
- Luke 4:1–13
- Luke 22:39–44
- James 1:2–12

Opening Our Eyes

It's ironic in these days of sophisticated technology and multiple means of communication that there still can be so much confusion in this world. This lack of clarity can crop up in many diverse situations. On one occasion, I had been driving home through a rural part of England. Emerging from a small town, I approached a crossroads. Not having any satellite navigation equipment in my (old) vehicle, I was dependent upon a road atlas and road signs. However, at this location there was no road sign as it was a new road and unmarked on the map. Fortunately, in answer to a prayer of bewilderment, God brought my attention to the sun visible in the southern sky. Needing to head south to London, I therefore decided to take the road towards the sun, eventually arriving at a major road (with road signs), thus ending my confusion!

Of course, Habakkuk's confusion regarding events in his nation was of much greater impact. He had recounted to God the appalling behaviour that he was witnessing around him, which God had seemed initially unresponsive about. When He finally did reply, God told him that the might of the Babylonian Empire was about to be unleashed upon the powerless nation of Judah. This subsequently took place in 586 BC, eventually resulting in the mass deportation of the nation's inhabitants, the destruction of the Temple and the walls of Jerusalem.

The Babylonians

But Habakkuk was horror-struck at this information that the Jews were about to be disciplined by way of the Babylonians. This people's power and ruthlessness were renowned in that age. Their godlessness and hubris was also well known. God spelt that out when telling Habakkuk what He was about to oversee: 'they sweep past like the wind and go on – guilty people, whose own strength is their god' (Hab. 1:11).

It was this aspect regarding the Babylonian's own rejection of God that generated the most confusion within Habakkuk. How could God allow godless people to flourish? Why was evil being directed at God's own people? How could they survive this crushing and dark power? So the prophet returned with a second complaint. It's as though he's verbalising the facts that he knows about God and putting them alongside what he's now been told. The ensuing confusion was evident. What the Lord was about to put into motion simply did not match up to His character.

God's character

There were particular qualities about God that Habakkuk correctly drew out. The prophet knew that these factors were non-negotiable, starting with the Lord being eternal – from everlasting to everlasting – and thereby self-existent. This was important since the Babylonians were an emerging 'superpower' who'd overcome the previous Assyrian 'top dogs'. So, sooner or later (as proved to be the case) these Babylonians would themselves disappear. However, God would always be God, powerful enough to appoint those oppressors for their role, but also dependable (hence describing Him as 'my Rock'). Also described were God's holiness, purity and intolerance of wrong (Hab. 1:12–13). It was this last point that really perplexed the prophet on account of those Babylonians clearly being so wicked.

Although confused, Habakkuk's response in stating these qualities about God was a vital step in moving towards a place of confident trust. He had not yet found a firm footing but, even in complaining (again!), a necessary foundation was laid.

Discussion Starters

1. Habakkuk reminded God of His character and attributes. What is the value for ourselves in learning more about God's qualities?

_____

_____

_____

_____

_____

2. In connection with question one, what are the practical ways by which we can learn more about God's attributes?

_____

_____

_____

_____

_____

3. In response to confusion and trouble, what words are used in Psalm 31 to describe God? How can these images help us?

_____

_____

_____

_____

_____

4. Psalm 31 records a previous occasion when God's help was experienced. What is the value of being reminded of God's past intervention when feeling confused?

_____

_____

_____

_____

_____

5. What was the particular cause of the writer's confusion described in Psalm 77? How can this relate to ourselves?

_____

_____

_____

_____

_____

6. What action did the writer of Psalm 77 take in order to resolve his confusion? In what ways can that action be applied to our own situations when we are confused in our faith?

_____

_____

_____

_____

_____

7. What does James say about trouble and confusion that helps us understand situations we face (James 1)?

_____

_____

_____

_____

_____

8. According to James 1:3–4, what part does perseverance play when we are faced with trials and our faith in God is tested?

_____

_____

_____

_____

_____

Personal Application

Not one of us will escape or avoid the kind of perplexity that confronted Habakkuk. We are likely, if not already, to encounter situations we don't understand, and which conflict with our beliefs concerning the nature and work of God. But, like the prophet, our confidence in God can start to be re-established as we remind ourselves of His character and qualities.

Seeing Jesus in the Scriptures

When Jesus was tempted in the wilderness, He was subjected to particular attack. Satan threw doubts and confusion at Him regarding both His identity and purpose. Those questions with the repeated preface, 'If you are the Son of God...' (Luke 4:3,9) and the enticing offer, 'If you worship me, it will all be yours' (v7), were designed to derail Jesus' confidence in His Father. His retort was to repeat the declarations of Scripture regarding the provision and attributes of God.

At the end of His ministry at Gethsemane and Calvary, again undergoing attack that seemed designed to bring confusion, Jesus showed the humanity that He shared with us. The Gospel writers record: 'And being in anguish, he prayed more earnestly, and his sweat was like drops of blood falling to the ground' (Luke 22:44). 'Jesus cried out in a loud voice... "My God, my God, why have you forsaken me?"' (Matt. 27:46). But His ultimate confidence in God was subsequently revealed: 'yet not my will, but yours be done' (Luke 22:42). 'Father, into your hands I commit my spirit' (Luke 23:46).

WEEK FOUR

Commitment

Icebreaker

Think about the different occasions over the past week in which you've had to wait for something to happen before you can move forward. What factors affect our degree of control while we wait?

Bible Readings

- Habakkuk 2:1
- Psalm 27:13–14
- Psalm 130
- Lamentations 3:19–27
- Acts 1:1–11

Opening Our Eyes

There is a story of a theology professor who was found in an agitated state, pacing up and down his study. When asked what the trouble was, he replied: 'The trouble is that I'm in a hurry, but God is not!'

Many of us can identify with that comment and the inference that there are unavoidable occasions when we have to wait. The drive to get things done, actively press on, find answers and resolve issues is commonplace. Instant communications and technological resources at our fingertips add impetus to this kind of expectation. Making progress and being proactive is seen, even in church life, as being essential.

Habakkuk, as recorded in chapter 1, seemed to have been someone who quickly engaged in what was taking place. Having observed, with considerable anguish, the injustice, oppression and godlessness around him in the nation, he complained to God. The totally surprising response from the Lord, informing the prophet of His intention to allow the evil and repressive Babylonian empire to overrun Judah, met with a seemingly immediate reply. Habakkuk's further complaint about God's character not being consistent with this proposed action was, nevertheless, beginning to focus the prophet on the Lord.

Standing

The timespan that occupied that interchange between Habakkuk and God is not recorded. But what was stated is the prophet's next step: 'I will stand at my watch' (Hab. 2:1). It is not clear whether he literally climbed to the heights of a watchtower on the walls surrounding Jerusalem. But those few words described an important action and vital attitude. He made the decision to stand and wait. The original Hebrew word for 'stand' meant simply to 'stand fast,' or 'stand still'. Action and conversation on the part of Habakkuk now ceased. Part of that activity to simply 'stand' involved deliberately removing himself from the distracting and diverging views of other people around him. Figuratively or otherwise, he placed himself in isolation.

Looking

However, it was not sufficient for Habakkuk to find 'space'. There was a very positive reason for his action. Although he stood, he also looked: 'I will look to see' (v1). The prophet may now have been waiting for God to respond to his cry of perplexity, but it was with a proactive stance. That picture of him standing up on the rampart (watchtower) suggested that he was straining his eyes on the horizon for signs of activity. The original word meant 'to look out', and being 'watchful'. Everything else had been put to one side to enable him to be 'focused' (a fashionable word in the twenty-first century!).

Expecting

Hard experience tells us, however, that such 'waiting' is an activity that can be undertaken in vain. Our expectations do not always materialise. So the stance that Habakkuk took as he waited is, again, worth noting. He was certain that his waiting would result in a positive outcome: 'what he [the Lord] will say to me' (v1). This was in contrast to his opening complaint in which he accused God of not listening (see Hab. 1:2)! He'd achieved a complete turnaround, encouraged by God's answer on that earlier occasion, and was determined to understand what God was intending to accomplish through those confusing events.

So again there is a trace of confidence that Habakkuk was displaying. As he deliberately and resolutely chose to look to God, the prophet was choosing to trust God – to go His way – even as he simply waited.

Discussion Starters

1. What do we consider were the specific benefits of Habakkuk getting to a place where he could, 'look to see what he will say to me,' (Hab. 2:1) and how applicable are these benefits to us?

_____

_____

_____

_____

_____

2. What were the pressures that Habakkuk was facing, and how were they likely to prevent him from waiting expectantly for God's response?

_____

_____

_____

_____

_____

3. What are the kinds of difficulties that we are likely to face in trying to wait for God to speak and direct us?

_____

_____

_____

_____

_____

4. Psalm 130 described the psalmist's feelings as he looked to God. What qualities about God encouraged him as he did this, and how can they help us?

_____

_____

_____

_____

_____

5. The psalmist's view of God brought out in Psalm 27 resulted in him feeling confident (Psa. 27:13–14). What did he say about God that encouraged him in that respect?

_____

_____

_____

_____

_____

6. Jesus specifically instructed His followers to wait for His Spirit to come upon them. What was likely to have encouraged them to obey Him despite their confusion (see Acts 1:1–11)?

_____

_____

_____

_____

_____

7. What encouraged the writer of Lamentations to wait for God (Lam. 3:19–27)?

_____

_____

_____

_____

_____

8. In what ways can 'waiting' on God be evidence of having confidence and trust in Him?

_____

_____

_____

_____

_____

Personal Application

Habakkuk made the decision to get away from other people (literally or figuratively) and their potentially distracting influence in order to totally focus on God alone. This probably contrasts with our own experience and church practice. But spending time with God can be essential in helping us be open to God, who promises to speak to us. The psalmist expressed his confidence that God would respond: 'In the morning, LORD, you hear my voice; in the morning I lay my requests before you and wait expectantly' (Psa. 5:3). This encourages us also to have a resolute attitude and confidence in waiting before God.

Seeing Jesus in the Scriptures

Jesus' ministry on this earth followed many years of preparation and waiting. The Gospel writer, Luke, stated that during that time, 'Jesus grew in wisdom and stature, and in favour with God and man' (Luke 2:52), commencing His work only when He, 'was about thirty years old' (Luke 3:23). In the course of the three years that followed, there were occasions when it was particularly recorded that He separated Himself from other people in order to pray. These were sometimes all-night sessions, indicative of Him waiting for His Father to speak to Him (Matt. 14:13,23; 26:36-39; Mark 1:35; 6:46). Luke emphasised this trait of Jesus, like Habakkuk, to be determinedly focusing on God: 'But Jesus often withdrew to lonely places and prayed' (Luke 5:16).

WEEK FIVE

Changed perspective

Icebreaker

Most high-profile sports competitions involve some form of final to determine the ultimate winner or champion. As a group, discuss what different factors would influence the speculation and analysis regarding potential winners.

Bible Readings

- Habakkuk 2:2–20
- Mark 5:21–43
- Romans 1:17
- 2 Corinthians 5:7
- Galatians 3:11
- Hebrews 10:37–38

Opening Our Eyes

'Don't tell the score in the middle of the ball game' is an American expression relating to sport and warns against anticipating the result when only halfway through a match. It means that a supporter should not be pessimistic if their team is losing at half-time unless, like me, you follow a poorly performing club in the lower levels of the English Football League!

Habakkuk had received a horrendous message from God regarding the nation of Judah. This was infinitely worse than any sporting scenario. The Babylonian Empire was about to unleash its relentless invading forces upon them. But the prophet had committed himself to wait and look for God's response to the complaint that this action (which God was allowing) was inconsistent with His character. The reply that God gave was similar to that sporting expression: what Habakkuk was about to witness was *not* the final outcome.

Babylonian nemesis

Following these opening verses, God described the ultimate overthrow and destruction of the Babylonians. Although they were to be used to bring severe correction to God's wayward people, they would not be allowed to do so for any length of time. History confirmed this to be the case as the Babylonians subsequently met their nemesis by way of the emerging Persian Empire in 539 BC.

Action

However, this termination of Babylonian repression was to take place about 60 years in the future. So as far as Habakkuk was concerned, it was still 'half-time'. What did God say at this point to bring a change of perspective? Three aspects of His instructions were particularly important in developing Habakkuk's confidence in God. The first of these was action: the prophet was to hold on.

To facilitate this he was told to write down what God had said so that an accurate record was maintained, which would act as a reminder (Hab. 2:2). God underlined that the forthcoming change would not be immediate. The 'second-half' would be a long one! God's direction was clear: 'Though it linger, wait for it; it will certainly come and will not delay' (Hab. 2:3).

Attitude

But God also spoke to Habakkuk about the attitude that needed to be adopted while he waited. It was to be one of particularly trusting God. 'But the righteous person will live by his faithfulness' (Hab. 2:4). This was in marked contrast to the self-reliance of those invaders. Five successive 'woes' from God upon the Babylonians showed their misplaced reliance. This emphasis on the need for a 'righteous person' to 'live by his faithfulness' by putting their confidence in God was so fundamental that the apostle Paul quoted it when writing to other Christians (see Rom. 1:17; Gal. 3:11; also Heb. 10: 37–38). As Paul explained, a right relationship with God – and one that was ongoing – was only possible by trusting in Him.

Assurance

Finally, God also brought Habakkuk assurance of His power. This involved the fact that God would ultimately 'win'. 'For the earth will be filled with the knowledge of the glory of the LORD' (Hab. 2:14). The world would not be dominated by any human empire but by God. Connected with this was the Lord being in His holy temple, indicative of His total power and authority. There was only one response to that fact: 'let all the earth be silent before him' (Hab. 2:20). This series of revelations from God was aimed at changing Habakkuk's perspective, enabling him to have greater confidence in God in difficult times.

Discussion Starters

1. What purpose was being served by God in not revealing to Habakkuk the entire picture (especially concerning the eventual demise of the Babylonians) at the outset?

_____

_____

_____

_____

_____

2. Why did God speak out those five 'woes' against the Babylonians?

_____

_____

_____

_____

_____

3. Why was it so important that Habakkuk write down that message from God? What value is there in recording the things that we sense that God is speaking to us?

_____

_____

_____

_____

_____

4. What kinds of pressures in life, similar to Habakkuk's, can prevent us from being able to, 'live by faith, not by sight' (2 Cor. 5:7)?

_____

_____

_____

_____

_____

5. What factors would have made it difficult for Jairus to grasp that, when informed of his daughter's death, this was *not* the end (see Mark 5:21–43)?

_____

_____

_____

_____

_____

6. Which factors in the above question would also have applied to Habakkuk when learning about the Babylonian invasion, and what additional ones may have existed?

_____

_____

_____

_____

_____

7. What other examples are recorded in the Bible of God speaking into people's lives when things looked to be coming to an end?

_____

_____

_____

_____

_____

8. Why did God bring that closing instruction to Habakkuk about needing to be silent before Him (Hab. 2:20)? How does that apply to ourselves?

_____

_____

_____

_____

_____

Personal Application

Our world is full of uncertainties and the effects of 'hidden' agendas, particularly in the areas of politics and finance. Some are more pressing than others. There is a tendency to draw conclusions from our present experiences with regard to the future and what will happen. But the lesson that God showed Habakkuk also applies to ourselves in understanding that He has ultimate control and authority. Although adverse circumstances may seem inevitable and irreversible, He wants our perspective to change and for us to place our trust in Him. The apostle Paul underlined this need for confidence in God: 'For we live by faith, not by sight' (2 Cor. 5:7).

Seeing Jesus in the Scriptures

Jesus was frequently encountering people whose situations looked totally bleak and held no future hope. Jairus was a synagogue leader whose young daughter was dying. He came to ask Jesus to put His hand on her so that she would be healed and live. But en route to his house, they were delayed. Consequently, by the time their journey was resumed, a message was received that the daughter's condition had deteriorated and that she was now dead. However, Jesus' response to this terrible news was, 'Don't be afraid; just believe' (Mark 5:36). Jairus was being brought to see that this situation was not the end. Just as God spoke hope to Habakkuk in encouraging him to trust, so Jesus spoke hope to Jairus before speaking resurrection life to his 12-year-old child.

WEEK SIX

Considering the past

Icebreaker

Compile a list of the different types of media that you have used to record past events experienced by yourself and your family. Discuss which of these methods evoke the most vivid memories for you now, and why they do so.

Bible Readings

- Habakkuk 3:1–15
- Psalm 77
- Psalm 103
- Philippians 1:6
- 1 Corinthians 11:23–26
- Hebrews 13:5–8

Opening Our Eyes

The London 'Crossrail' route, linking the east and west suburbs of London, was a major undertaking. Huge tunnelling machines burrowed a path with millimetre precision through the clay soil under the city. But although technical innovation was evident, these railway tunnels also made use of existing infrastructure. When digging 'Crossrail', stretches of old tunnel near the Thames were incorporated into the route. Robust Victorian engineering from the past was a vital contribution to this network of the future.

Habakkuk had been devastated by the news that the Babylonian Empire was to be used in bringing correction to the people of Judah. Although God had then revealed to the prophet that this was not the end – these ruthless invaders would themselves eventually be vanquished – Habakkuk was still reeling from the implications. He was struggling with the obvious terrible consequences of this oppression, and having to reconcile this with the assurance that God had the final say in unfolding events.

Prayer

It was in the context of grappling with conflicting emotions that Habakkuk turned to God again. He knew that he needed to trust God. But his confidence was still not high. So he prayed to God as described at the start of chapter 3. However, there was a marked change in his approach. He had previously talked to God about the state of His people and the horrors of those invaders. Now he talked to God about God Himself.

Those other issues, however much they burdened the prophet, were put to one side. He now wanted to focus only on God, starting by referring to God's 'fame' and His 'deeds'. The former had been 'heard' while in respect of the latter Habakkuk was in 'awe'. But this immediately generated a request, asking God to, 'Repeat them in our day'. The King James version puts it as: 'revive thy work in the midst of the years' (Hab. 3:2, KJV). This rendition places an emphasis on Habakkuk wanting God to intervene when there was an apparent lull in His activity, as contrasted with the very evident Babylonian threat.

Past

Habakkuk's prayer then moved on to recount some particular occasions when God *had* intervened in the past. As with 'Crossrail', a basis for the future rested on events in the past. It featured the Israelites facing enormous odds when experiencing deliverance from Egyptian slavery (Hab. 3:5), escaping through the Red Sea (vv8,10,15), travelling across the desert, and fighting in the Promised Land (vv7,13).

Power

These had been key events in Israel's history. They were also times when God's power had been vividly displayed. Most prominent was when the 'Sun and moon stood still in the heavens' (Hab. 3:11). This related to the incident when Joshua, undertaking a 'mopping up' role in the Promised Land, seemed to need more daylight in order to complete military operations. So God, in some way, facilitated the delay of nightfall by stopping the celestial bodies (Josh. 10:9–14)!

However, God's power was revealed in other ways: 'Plague went before him... shook the earth... made the nations tremble... The ancient mountains crumbled' (Hab. 3:5–6). Habakkuk recounted what God had supernaturally undertaken in the past because he wanted God again 'In wrath [to] remember mercy' (Hab. 3:2). This prayer was an important means in continuing to help Habakkuk choose to trust God despite what was happening around him.

Discussion Starters

1. What causes us to be more focused on our troubles than on God?

_____

_____

_____

_____

_____

2. How can we more easily concentrate on God and His sovereign power when praying?

_____

_____

_____

_____

_____

3. What are the positive features at the start of Psalm 103 that can bring encouragement when we face adversity?

_____

_____

_____

_____

_____

4. Psalm 103 includes reminders of God's attitude towards us. In what ways do these embolden us as we pray?

_____

_____

_____

_____

_____

5. In what ways can the statements of God's continued and unchanging work in our lives spur us on (see Phil. 1:6; Heb. 13:8)?

_____

_____

_____

_____

_____

6. A positive step is described in Psalm 77 regarding the writer choosing to focus on God's miracles of the past (Psa. 77:10–12). Why is it important to remember that God performs miracles?

_____

_____

_____

_____

_____

7. What is the difference between 'remembering' and 'meditating' as described in Psalm 77? What is the value of the latter?

_____

_____

_____

_____

_____

8. How do miracles help us have a clearer glimpse of God's glory, and why is this important (Hab. 3:3–7)?

_____

_____

_____

_____

_____

Personal Application

God wants us to pray about our burdens. The writer to the Hebrews brought this encouragement: 'Let us then approach the throne of grace with confidence, so that we may receive mercy and find grace to help us in our time of need' (Heb. 4:16). However, as Habakkuk showed, even in talking to God about our circumstances we need to link that with declarations about God's splendour and power as evidenced in the past. The psalmist was aware of this approach. Although under attack and threatened he chose to focus on God, not his adversity: 'I will consider all your works and meditate on all your mighty deeds. Your ways, God, are holy. What god is as great as our God?' (Psa. 77:12–13).

Seeing Jesus in the Scriptures

Jesus instituted 'The Lord's supper' (described by the apostle Paul) consisting of bread and wine being consumed, 'in remembrance' of Him (see 1 Cor. 11:24, 25). Those representations were the means of vividly looking back at the cross and remembering the suffering that He underwent for our salvation. This was to be a present and continuing reassurance of Jesus' unending love to be undertaken, 'until he comes' (1 Cor. 11:26). Jesus' death was actually foreshadowed many years previously by the slaughter of the Passover Lamb prior to the Exodus, the latter being referenced by Habakkuk in his prayer (Hab. 3:5).

WEEK SEVEN

Confidence

Icebreaker

Look at a current national or local newspaper and consider your reactions to the various headlines (the articles that immediately attract your attention as well as those you might otherwise ignore). Discuss what causes those different reactions.

Bible Readings

- Habakkuk 3:16–19
- 2 Chronicles 20:1–30
- Proverbs 3:5–6
- Hebrews 12:1–3

Opening Our Eyes

Chariots of Fire is the well known film depicting the achievements of Eric Liddell. On account of his Christian convictions, he had refused to compete in the 100 metre sprint competition at the 1924 Paris Olympics as the heats were to take place on a Sunday. Although the favourite to win that event, he instead ran the 400 metres. Unexpectedly, he achieved first place and won the coveted gold. However, the film does not describe subsequent events. Eric Liddell's passion was to serve God as a missionary in China. So in 1925 he left his native Scotland, engaging in work for God in an increasingly hostile and unstable environment arising from the Sino-Japanese war. Eventually, in 1941, Liddell was interned by the Japanese along with other missionaries and westerners, subsequently dying in an internment camp.

The feelings and emotions that Eric Liddell felt as the inevitability of internment became apparent have not been disclosed. Perhaps they were like Habakkuk's back in around 586 BC. God had told the prophet that the Babylonian army was about to overrun the country of Judah. In the aftermath, God's people would be captured and taken into forced exile. Although Habakkuk was assured that this Babylonian domination would only be temporary, and determined to focus on God, he was only human. This was apparent when he recorded: 'I heard and my heart pounded, my lips quivered at the sound; decay crept into my bones, and my legs trembled' (Hab. 3:16). This was his response to the, 'day of calamity,' that was inevitably approaching.

Confrontation

Habakkuk's response did not seem positive. But, again, he was facing up to the reality of what he was feeling. He also confronted the physical likelihood of future events. These were vividly described: 'the fig-tree does not bud… no grapes on the vines… olive crop fails… fields produce no food… no sheep in the sheepfold… no cattle in the stalls' (Hab. 3:17). Yet this confrontation was a necessary step to his next action. He was not pretending that things might be different, or glossing over them. This was an acknowledgement that what God said *would* happen.

Confidence

But this confrontation then moved to confidence. Habakkuk's viewpoint was that, as shown in the history of God's people, God had the final say. Those memorable events previously rehearsed by the prophet concerning the Exodus, crossing the Red Sea, and deliverance from impossible odds (Hab. 3:3–15) were proof of that fact. It was this understanding that enabled Habakkuk to praise God, specifically describing Him as Saviour (Hab. 3:18).

Climbing

However, Habakkuk didn't stop at this point. He further realised that God could enable him to climb above the circumstances and confusion that had enveloped him at a physical and emotional level. 'He enables me to tread on the heights' (v19) meant that God was giving him a broader and higher perspective. The prophet was able to see events as God saw them – at least within the confines of his immediate context. This, in turn, gave him even greater confidence, describing God as 'Sovereign' (v19) being in control of this earth in general, and His people in particular. Both the preface and appendix to this chapter indicated that the content had a musical element. This was fitting, since being able to 'rejoice' and be 'joyful' (v18) in God could be expressed in tuneful ways in which we can also join as we also look to God in confident expectation.

Discussion Starters

1. Why is it important that, like Habukkuk, we do not gloss over emerging situations that are likely to be difficult?

_____

_____

_____

_____

_____

2. What does Habakkuk's response to unfolding events teach us regarding our own possible reactions to daunting situations?

_____

_____

_____

_____

_____

3. How can the recollection of previous interventions from God in terms of Him having the final say, either as described in the Bible or our own past experience, be of help to us?

_____

_____

_____

_____

_____

4. What does the account of King Jehoshaphat's response to bad news, and his subsequent action, teach us in respect of dealing with overwhelming circumstances (2 Chron. 20:1–4)?

_____

_____

_____

_____

5. In what way was King Jehoshaphat's response similar to Habakkuk's and also a lesson for us (2 Chron. 20:5–13)?

_____

_____

_____

_____

_____

6. What generated confidence within King Jehoshaphat (2 Chron. 20:14-19)? How does this relate to us?

_____

_____

_____

_____

_____

7. Both Habakkuk and King Jehoshaphat showed their confidence in God by praising Him. What was the content and significance of this praise (2 Chron. 20:20–21)?

_____

_____

_____

_____

_____

8. Why is praise to God an expression of our confidence in Him as shown by Habakkuk?

_____

_____

_____

_____

_____

Personal Application

It is important to understand that our perspective regarding the situations and circumstances that we face is an incomplete one. We are likely to have a warped or restricted picture of what is actually going on because of our human limitations. This is why we need to focus on God, reminding ourselves of His love and power. In doing so we grow in confidence as we begin to grasp His unfailing goodness. This confidence is well founded, as the writer of Proverbs underlines: 'Trust in the LORD with all your heart and lean not on your own understanding; in all your ways submit to him, and he will make your paths straight' (Prov. 3:5–6).

Seeing Jesus in the Scriptures

The writer to the Hebrews pointed to the one who looked forward with confidence even though for Him, as for Habakkuk, the immediate future was bleak. We are encouraged to run the race, 'fixing our eyes on Jesus, the pioneer and perfecter of faith. For the joy that was set before him he endured the cross, scorning its shame, and sat down at the right hand of the throne of God' (Heb. 12:2). Also like Habakkuk, the writer then used this demonstration of Jesus' confidence as a means of moving on: 'Consider him who endured such opposition from sinners, so that you will not grow weary and lose heart' (Heb. 12:3).

Leader's Notes

Week One: Complaining

Icebreaker

Banks, holiday companies, energy suppliers and telecommunications networks probably form the majority of organisations with which we have contact and to whom we may have cause to complain. Written or emailed complaints are the normal ways of raising issues.

Aim of the session

To be aware that we can talk to God about all of our feelings and circumstances.

Discussion Starters

1. Our own approach to prayer may be influenced by reading prayers of renowned Christians and hearing prayers that are led at church services. However, Habakkuk's prayer showed that, among other factors, spontaneous prayer from the heart (or emotions) is also heard and accepted by God. This informal approach was nevertheless undergirded with a sense of reverence.

2. Habakkuk was clearly aware of the wrongs that were taking place around him. He did not pretend that they didn't exist or ignore them. Further, he was not immune from the negative feelings and frustrations they created in him as he observed the suffering people in his community.

3. Behind the complaints in Psalm 142 were the emotions that the psalmist felt of being alone, uncared for and victimised. The NIV heading, 'When he was in the cave' indicated that he was physically and emotionally isolated. The emotive words that were used to describe this condition brought that sense of reality regarding his complaint to God. Our circumstances may be very different but we can identify with his feeling of isolation.

4. The sense of powerlessness produces the realisation that resolution can only arise from outside help. Ultimately, of course, only God can provide this for us. For the psalmist it was therefore a further step towards God, linked with an honesty regarding human inadequacy to effect change.

5. The practical mechanics of the psalmist's prayer ('cry aloud', 'lift my voice', 'pour out', Psa. 142:1–2; 'cry' Psa. 142:5–6) point to his wholehearted approach to God, which we can emulate. He also verbalised his honest assessment regarding his isolation and dependence upon God for help (Psa. 142:4–7). These all contributed to having the sense of being 'real' with God.

6. The big difference between these complaints of God's people at the time of Isaiah, and those of Habakkuk and the psalmist, was that the former were talking among themselves and not to God. The nature of their complaint was that God didn't seem to be aware or interested in their situation. So God, by drawing attention to this complaint, showed this not to be the case.

7.   The contrast that God brought in respect of that complaint was that He was omnipotent and that the idols which had been set up were lifeless and powerless. God also pointed to His majestic power in creating the heavens and overseeing all that happens on this earth, thereby helping His people see that they could choose to trust in Him.

8.   Jeremiah, the author of Lamentations, prophesied at a time when God's people were facing invasion by the Babylonians (as God was to tell Habakkuk in the next verses). The complaint arising from this destruction failed to recognise that sin had brought this upon the nation. Jeremiah pointed out that the only option the people had was to examine themselves and return to God. We are also faced with choices when complaining: to direct them to God and reflect upon our behaviour as being a possible reason for our troubles or to carry on moaning.

Week Two: Caught out

Icebreaker

The surprise element may arise because of the identity of the person from whom the gift came, or that it met an undisclosed need. It may also have been given at an unexpected time.

Aim of the session

To be alert to God's unexpected intervention.

Discussion Starters

1. God wanted Habakkuk to be fully aware of what was about to take place. The prophet was to have no misapprehension regarding the identity or evil character of the empire that was to bring severe discipline to Judah. Similarly we need to face up to surrounding wickedness, neither ignoring nor belittling it, being certain that God is knowledgeable about all situations.

2. The response from God to Habakkuk was prefaced: 'Look at the nations and watch – and be utterly amazed... I am going to do something... that you would not believe, even if you were told' (Hab. 1:5). These were big hints to prepare for something unexpected! Isaiah 55 and Ephesians 3 alert us to the fact that we have limited understanding of God's 'big picture'.

3. Gideon's response to God's call to lead the Israelites against their invaders was to refer to his family, his own low standing and tribal background (only half of them had been committed enough to enter the Promised Land). However, God was not put off by Gideon's seeming lack of credentials; neither is He put off by ours.

4. Gideon, having responded to God, issued a call to arms to various tribes of Israel. Although facing an enormous enemy army, God told Gideon that the number of Israelite men assembled was too many. It was eventually whittled down to just 300, God making it clear that He was able to bring victory using a negligible number. Similarly, God can use our small resources to amazing effect.

5. Ananias faced up to what he knew about the situation. His response to God's surprising call for him to go and restore sight to Saul was to recount the harsh facts that this man was an enemy of God's people with powers to arrest and harm them. His obedience in following God's instruction showed the importance of responding even when God doesn't seem to make sense.

6. The church had been 'earnestly praying to God' (Acts 12:5) for Peter, who'd been imprisoned pending execution. God dramatically intervened so that he escaped. He turned up at the front door of Mary's house where people had met to pray for him. But when the servant who'd answered the door announced that Peter was outside, she was told that she was 'out of her mind', or that it was Peter's 'angel'. God surprised those Christians by answering their prayers, although clearly not prayed with much faith.

7. Our expectations regarding the type of people who could become Christians can, sadly, be similar to secular employers recruiting staff based on good qualifications. Paul drew attention to the fact that God's choice was surprisingly different: He chooses the 'foolish', 'weak', 'lowly' and 'despised' (1 Cor. 1:27–28). This was so that no one could boast that they had qualities which merited God's call. So we need to be careful against making assumptions regarding those with whom we aim to share the gospel.

8. Paul's own response regarding God's awesome power was to 'kneel before the Father' (Eph. 3:14). He then prayed that Christians might be strengthened and grasp something of the immensity of God's love. This points us to the need to be open to what God does and how He works, which is likely to be outside of our expectations.

Week Three: Confusion

Icebreaker

Many factors can arise to affect a planned journey. Weather conditions, mechanical failure, outside incidents, mistakes and other issues can bring confusion and delay.

Aim of the session

To see that although we may be confused by what God does, He can still be trusted.

Discussion Starters

1. Relationships with people are deepened as time is spent together, conversations take place, and tasks are jointly undertaken. In the same way, making an effort to learn more about God, His character and ability, brings us closer to Him and increases our trust. Both Abraham and Moses were described as 'friends' of God arising from intimacy (Exod. 33:11; 2 Chron. 20:7).

2. Practical steps to be taken to learn more about God include those of regular Bible reading and talking (and listening) to Him in prayer. The Gospel accounts highlight God's character revealed through Jesus, who stated: 'My food… is to do the will of Him who sent me and to finish his work' (John 4:34). Arising from these, stepping out in faith to serve Him helps build up our trust. The apostle Paul also instructs us to 'be filled with the Spirit' (Eph. 5:18); the work of the Spirit is to guide us into 'all the truth' (John 16:13).

3. The various images of God (including 'rock of refuge', 'fortress'; Psa. 31:2) help reinforce the fact that He is the dependable and strong protector in

our state of helplessness and uncertainty. The writer of the psalm encourages us to 'hope in the LORD' (v24), not looking to our own ability but to God's.

4. Reminders of God's past interventions in times of stress and confusion (described in Psa. 31:21–22) help build confidence in Him. This is both in terms of recognising His willingness to respond to our 'cry for mercy', and His willingness to do so: 'showed me the wonders of His love' (Psa. 31:21).

5. The psalmist held a similar viewpoint to Habakkuk's, particularly his initial one of believing that God no longer cared or wanted to intervene (Psa. 77:7–9; Hab. 1:2–3). This had been the outcome of his distress of an undisclosed origin (Psa. 77:1–2). Our response in times of pressure can similarly be that of confusion and uncertainty – God not seeming to be active in accordance with His character.

6. The psalmist described himself as stopping and taking stock: 'Then I thought' (Psa. 77:10). He didn't hold any immediate answers to his confusion but sensed that dwelling upon negative thoughts was not helpful. He then reflected on his past experiences of God's intervention, His care and power. In the same way our recall concerning God's answers to prayer and past help are steps in replacing confusion with trust.

7. The key verse is James 1:2 – 'trials of many kinds' – a reminder that confusion is but one type of trial with which we will have to contend. Underlying this are the facts that we undoubtedly will face trials, there is no quick or easy solution, and that God is aware of our situation. James actually states that God wants us to consider these with an attitude of 'pure joy'.

8. The 'pure joy' referred to above is not arising from the trials themselves, but what they can achieve. This is stated as being 'perseverance' (James 1:3–4,12), which leads to maturity. Wisdom is needed to understand the steps we need to take and trust we need to maintain.

Week Four: Commitment

Icebreaker

Factors affecting our degree of control (or impatience!) might include the amount of information we hold, external pressures, having a 'driven' personality, or simply wanting to move on.

Aim of the session

To understand the steps enabling us to wait with a godly attitude.

Discussion Starters

1. Habakkuk was conscious of being confronted with a developing situation, foretold by God, which was confusing. Importantly, he knew that no one else could help bring any understanding. Only in coming to God could Habakkuk receive the clarity he sought. Even the internet in our own age doesn't have all the answers! God invites us to come to Him and learn His perspective on situations (Jer. 33:3).

2. Habakkuk described an overwhelming awareness of the evil coming from the Babylonians and a sense of acute powerlessness ('swallow up'; Hab. 1:13). In addition he could not see any outcome apart from disaster for God's people. A likely reaction was that of paralysing fear as recorded by David ('overwhelmed', 2 Sam. 22:5). Habakkuk recognised the need to step away from confusion, fear and other people, and to focus on God.

3.   Our own difficulties, similar to Habakkuk's in terms of being subjected to stress and overwhelming concerns (though not for the same reasons), are compounded by all the technologies that can feed our minds. The impact of the media in its different and persuasive forms can constitute a serious obstacle in detaching ourselves from what's around us in order to get close to God.

4.   God's ability to forgive sin and hear those who call to Him brought encouragement in terms of focusing on Him. These encouragements were intertwined with God's dependability ('in his word I put my hope'; Psa. 130:5). The psalmist saw sin as the root cause of his troubles. Like ourselves, experiencing God's 'unfailing love' (Psa. 130:7) was an incentive in wholeheartedly approaching Him ('my whole being waits'; Psa. 130:5).

5.   Psalm 27 described various attributes of God. These qualities included His approachability ('seek him in his temple'; Psa. 27:4), protection ('keep me safe'; Psa. 27:5), attentiveness ('Hear my voice'; Psa. 27:7) and being close ('the LORD will receive me'; Psa. 27:10).

6.   Jesus' resurrection from the grave and His promise of power when the Holy Spirit came subsequent to their waiting, would have brought encouragement despite confusion (Acts 1:6). They also experienced a supernatural visitation! Significantly, their waiting took the form of being, 'joined together constantly in prayer' (Acts 1:14).

7. The writer of Lamentations was actually caught up in the terrible destruction arising from the Babylonian invasion foretold to Habakkuk. But he was convinced of God's never-failing compassion being 'new every morning' (Lam. 3:23) and that he could place his hope in God's goodness (Lam. 3:24). This outlook meant that he could focus on God, who would work things out in the unpromising scenario that was being experienced (Lam. 3:25–26).

8. Like Habakkuk, who was facing the looming and physical threat of evil terror being unleashed on God's people, we may face very real and powerful pressures. But instead of allowing ourselves to be overwhelmed by such situations there is the choice, like Habakkuk, of focusing on God (however tentative this may feel). This shows that our confidence and trust are not so much directed towards ourselves or other people as towards God.

Week Five: Changed perspective

Icebreaker

Different factors influencing the analysis of a sports event would include past performance, recent results, 'expert' opinion and current fitness. But an 'underdog' can unexpectedly win!

Aim of the session

To understand the steps we can take to enable a godly perspective to be held.

Discussion Starters

1. God was working to develop in Habakkuk a deeper and more trusting relationship with Him. The prophet got closer to God as he persisted in responding to what was unfolding before him. It was the prerogative of God to disclose the details of the Babylonian demise. He chooses to bring revelation and understanding when it serves His purposes, showing that He has ultimate control, and to draw us closer to Him (see Gen. 18:16–33 when God spoke to Abraham).

2. The repeated prefacing of the word 'Woe' in respect of those Babylonians was to confirm the outcome of their evil and that God was implacably set against them. When it's recorded that God repeats something then it's usually indicating an emphasis. Joseph, many centuries earlier, had explained this to Pharaoh in respect of his dreams (Gen. 41:32).

3. God pointed out that the revelation regarding the downfall of the Babylonians was not going to take place in the immediate future: 'Though it linger' (Hab. 2:3). There would consequently be times when the daily grind of the ongoing situation would make it seem as though nothing was going to happen. If it was written down, it would therefore maintain hope and trust in God. This also applies to ourselves during times of waiting.

4. Habakkuk's reaction to physical threats to his safety and lifestyle could also relate to ourselves (though not from the same cause). The emotional effects of paralysing fear and hopelessness can also be factors that relate to us. The apostle Paul's instruction came on the back of his own experience of uncertainty and hardships.

5. Jairus had never witnessed anyone being raised from the dead and therefore had no personal precedent on which to base any hope. Although the Old Testament described God's interventions in this way, these had taken place centuries before Jairus and so lacked impact for him. He also had not grasped (if he had ever heard) the full implications of Jesus' proclamation at the outset of His ministry (Luke 4:18–19). The inevitability of death would have made it difficult for Jairus to see that anything could change.

6. Habakkuk had not personally witnessed God's great power being released in freeing His people from slavery and oppression. Like Jairus, his reference points were only the records of what others had written down. Further, the inevitability (in human terms) of the situation would have made it difficult to see anything differently. In Habakkuk's case there was also the aspect of God's people deserving this pending discipline.

7. Examples could include:
   • Moses – aged 80, having been a shepherd out in the desert for 40 years and seemingly beyond the point where he could be used again by God (Exod. 2);
   • Joseph – imprisoned in Egypt on false charges and beyond contact by his family (Gen. 39);
   • David – on the run and deposed as king by his son in a rebellion (2 Sam. 15).

8. Habakkuk, having fully voiced his complaints and confusion before God, needed to pay attention to what God was saying and planning. Being silent before Him was vital for that to take place. The psalmist also described God's instruction in that respect (Psa. 46:10).

Week Six: Considering the past

Icebreaker

Modern technology provides many ways by which events can be recorded. The more effective the visual and audio presentation, the greater and more absorbing the impact. However, even written details of events, especially those penned immediately afterwards, can have a powerful effect when considering the fact that they were etched perhaps many decades previously.

Aim of the session

Stress that what we undergo can easily dominate our ongoing thoughts and emotions. But reflecting on past experiences and the ways in which God has clearly stepped into our lives and circumstances is a means of pulling away from immediate pressures. It enables us to have a perspective where God has the deciding input.

Discussion Starters

1. We live in a culture in which our minds seem programmed to most readily pick up messages from visible and audible sources around us. Technology means that we are being continually bombarded with such powerful distorted messages (explicit or implicit) about ourselves and our world.

2. Prayer is the means by which we can shut out other voices and influences in order to focus on God. That's why a time and place of quiet, away from distraction, is important. Jesus is recorded as 'often' withdrawing to 'lonely places' to pray (Luke 5:16). Praying aloud and singing corporate worship to God are also aids in concentration.

3. The psalmist directs us to remember what God has done for us in the past when we were noticeably powerless to sort ourselves out. The words used in Psalm 103:3–5 ('forgives', 'heals', 'redeems', 'crowns', 'satisfies' and 'renewed') show God to be seriously hands-on even when we are not in a good place.

4. God is described in Psalm 103 as working positively in our lives even though fully aware of our condition and inclination: 'for he knows how we are formed, he remembers that we are dust' (Psa. 103:14). His fatherly compassion and care are the governing factors in His dealings with us, and can embolden us as we pray and face difficult situations.

5. Habakkuk asked God to 'revive' His work in 'the midst of the years' (Hab. 3:2; KJV), seeing the need for God's work to be completed; the Babylonian invasion was not the end of things. We can be stimulated in our journey of faith in knowing that God doesn't give up on us and has the ability and desire to bring us through.

6. Like Habakkuk and the psalmist, we can be overwhelmed by situations we cannot change or be unable to see things being any different. So it's important to realise that God is capable of changing things. He can make 'a way in the wilderness and streams in the wasteland' (Isa. 43:19).

7. Meditating is the act of continuing to remember as distinct from simply recalling a past event and then moving on. The original Hebrew word included the action of reflecting, contemplating and pondering. This means of recall helps to reinforce within us our trust in God who performs miracles, as He has done in the past.

8. The power and omnipotence of God as witnessed (and then remembered) in the form of miracles reflect something of His glory. Even though, like Habakkuk, we may be confronted by impossible and overwhelming situations, remembering God's miraculous power can help bring a totally different perspective and agenda.

Week Seven: Confidence

Icebreaker

As people, we respond to news and information in different ways at different times. On some occasions we may simply take things on board at a superficial level (not necessarily remembering them for any length of time), whereas other information may impact our emotions and, more deeply, our spirits.

Aim of the session

To see that our trust in God is evidenced but also strengthened by the action of praising Him.

Discussion Starters

1. Being genuine about difficult situations is important because sooner or later we are going to be impacted by events, whether or not we acknowledge them initially. Jesus clearly stated to His disciples: 'In this world you will have trouble' (John 16:33). Being a Christian does not exempt us from stress and problems in this life.

2. Habakkuk shows us that it's OK to be open about problems and their potential effects. Although he also shows that it's natural to respond emotionally to such situations, his example of turning to God illustrates that we don't have to remain in a state of turmoil. Thanks to our relationship with God, it's possible to have a different perspective that brings us to a place of peace, even though there might not be any outward change in circumstances.

3. Realising that God has the final say can bring a new dimension to pressing circumstances. While we may still have no influence to engineer any change or improvement, we can rest in God's wisdom and power to intervene. Believing prayer fuelled by remembering biblical accounts of God working in situations means that the mountains can be moved.

4. Jehoshaphat's initial reaction to the threat of invasion was of understandable alarm – if not actual panic! The crucial point was that he then took hold of himself ('resolved'; 2 Chron. 20:3). He 'got a grip' and did not allow his emotions to take control, knowing in his mind and spirit that he needed to bring to God the news that he had received. His action also included fasting and getting others alongside him.

5. Both Habakkuk and King Jehoshaphat not only turned to God in prayer, but talked to Him openly about the pressing situations they faced (even though God was already fully aware). They also both referred to God's previous interventions in the affairs of the nation together with reminders of His qualities and character. These are all factors that we can use when we come to God ourselves.

6. King Jehoshaphat had a significant confidence boost arising from God's very tangible and definitive

response. God's Spirit coming upon a Levite in that congregation and bringing the message to the king and the people was clearly described. Jesus explained that it is the work of the Holy Spirit to bring us into 'all truth' (John 16:13) and 'teach' (John 14:26) us about God and His ways. Through Him we can hear God's voice.

7. The singers who were appointed to lead the army were particularly highlighting God's holiness – that He is totally pure and undefiled in His nature, motives, thoughts, words and actions. They sung about God's love and mercy being constant and endless.

8. Praise to God is evidence of our trust in Him, even though immediate circumstances may not seem positive or provide a basis for hope. In praising God we are declaring His control over all things and that, in the end, He will be vindicated as Lord of all.

Notes...

Notes...

Latest Resources

The Popular *Cover to Cover* Bible Study Series

1 Corinthians
Growing a Spirit-filled church
ISBN: 978-1-85345-374-8

2 Corinthians
Restoring harmony
ISBN: 978-1-85345-551-3

1,2,3 John
Walking in the truth
ISBN: 978-1-78259-763-6

1 Peter
Good reasons for hope
ISBN: 978-1-78259-088-0

2 Peter
Living in the light of God's promises
ISBN: 978-1-78259-403-1

23rd Psalm
The Lord is my shepherd
ISBN: 978-1-85345-449-3

1 Timothy
*Healthy churches –
effective Christians*
ISBN: 978-1-85345-291-8

2 Timothy and Titus
Vital Christianity
ISBN: 978-1-85345-338-0

Abraham
Adventures of faith
ISBN: 978-1-78259-089-7

Acts 1-12
Church on the move
ISBN: 978-1-85345-574-2

Acts 13-28
To the ends of the earth
ISBN: 978-1-85345-592-6

Barnabas
Son of encouragement
ISBN: 978-1-85345-911-5

Bible Genres
Hearing what the Bible really says
ISBN: 978-1-85345-987-0

Daniel
Living boldly for God
ISBN: 978-1-85345-986-3

David
A man after God's own heart
ISBN: 978-1-78259-444-4

Ecclesiastes
*Hard questions and
spiritual answers*
ISBN: 978-1-85345-371-7

Elijah
A man and his God
ISBN: 978-1-85345-575-9

Elisha
A lesson in faithfulness
ISBN: 978-1-78259-494-9

Ephesians
Claiming your inheritance
ISBN: 978-1-85345-229-1

Esther
For such a time as this
ISBN: 978-1-85345-511-7

Ezekiel
A prophet for all times
ISBN: 978-1-78259-836-7

Fruit of the Spirit
Growing more like Jesus
ISBN: 978-1-85345-375-5

Galatians
Freedom in Christ
ISBN: 978-1-85345-648-0

God's Rescue Plan
*Finding God's fingerprints
on human history*
ISBN: 978-1-85345-294-9

Great Prayers of the Bible
Applying them to our lives today
ISBN: 978-1-85345-253-6

Habakkuk
Choosing God's way
ISBN: 978-1-78259-843-5

Haggai
Motivating God's people
ISBN: 978-1-78259-686-8

Hebrews
Jesus – simply the best
ISBN: 978-1-85345-337-3

Hosea
The love that never fails
ISBN: 978-1-85345-290-1

Isaiah 1-39
Prophet to the nations
ISBN: 978-1-85345-510-0

For current prices or to order, visit **www.cwr.org.uk/shop**
Available online or from Christian bookshops.

Be inspired by God.
Every day.

Confidently face life's challenges by equipping yourself daily with God's Word. There is something for everyone...

Every Day with Jesus

Selwyn Hughes' renowned writing is updated by Mick Brooks into these trusted and popular notes.

Life Every Day

Jeff Lucas helps apply the Bible to daily life through his trademark humour and insight.

Inspiring Women Every Day

Encouragement, uplifting scriptures and insightful daily thoughts for women.

The Manual

Straight-talking guide to help men walk daily with God. Written by Carl Beech.

To find out more about all our daily Bible reading notes, or to take out a subscription, visit **www.cwr.org.uk/biblenotes** or call 01252 784700. Also available in Christian bookshops.

 Printed format   Large print format   Email format  Ebook format

SmallGroup central

All of our small group ideas and resources in one place

Online:

www.smallgroupcentral.org.uk
is filled with free video teaching,
tools, articles and a whole host
of ideas.

On the road:

A range of seminars themed for
small groups can be brought to
your local community. Contact us at
hello@smallgroupcentral.org.uk

In print:

Books, study guides and DVDs
covering an extensive list of themes,
Bible books and life issues.

Find out more at:
www.smallgroupcentral.org.uk

Courses and events

Waverley Abbey College

Publishing and media

Conference facilities

Transforming lives

CWR's vision is to enable people to experience personal transformation through applying God's Word to their lives and relationships.

Our Bible-based training and resources help people around the world to:
• Grow in their walk with God
• Understand and apply Scripture to their lives
• Resource themselves and their church
• Develop pastoral care and counselling skills
• Train for leadership
• Strengthen relationships, marriage and family life and much more.

Our insightful writers provide daily Bible reading notes and other resources for all ages, and our experienced course designers and presenters have gained an international reputation for excellence and effectiveness.

CWR's Training and Conference Centre in Surrey, England, provides excellent facilities in an idyllic setting – ideal for both learning and spiritual refreshment.

CWR Applying God's Word
to everyday life and relationships

CWR, Waverley Abbey House,
Waverley Lane, Farnham,
Surrey GU9 8EP, UK

Telephone: **+44 (0)1252 784700**
Email: **info@cwr.org.uk**
Website: **www.cwr.org.uk**

Registered Charity No. 294387
Company Registration No. 1990308